# Upon the blue *Couch*

## LAURIE KOLP

*Winter Goose*
*Publishing*

Winter Goose Publishing
2701 Del Paso Road, 130-92
Sacramento, CA 95835

www.wintergoosepublishing.com
Contact Information: info@wintergoosepublishing.com

Upon the Blue Couch

COPYRIGHT © 2014 by Laurie Kolp

First Edition, March 2014

ISBN: 978-1-941058-08-4

Cover Art by Winter Goose Publishing
Typeset by Odyssey Books

Published in the United States of America

*For my mother, who passed away a few weeks before the book's publication;*
*and to my father who stood by her side. From them I learned the meaning*
*of true love, and as a result found mine.*

*My dear husband, Pete, and three children, Katie, Andrew, and Nicholas,*
*deserve just as much recognition,*
*for without their support, I could not have pulled this off.*

*My sister, Molly, has cheered me on, and for that I'm truly grateful.*

*Many thanks to my poetry friends, who are too many to list*
*(but they know who they are).*

*Jessica Kristie, and the editorial team at Winter Goose Publishing,*
*thank you for believing in me.*

# Contents

# Part I

# If You Paint My Picture

Color me silky smooth
with skin as pale
as buttermilk, a touch
of strawberry, a blush
when ruffled by a smartass.

Prepare for disarray—
chameleon eyes may
deviate from green,
reflecting tincture
of certain clothes I wear,
echoing autumn in my hair.

Get the iron out because creases
in expression distract, but go
unnoticed when I smile,
eyes drawn to tainted teeth—

make them movie-star white,
with plump lips painted red.

And the subtle scar
on my cleft chin,
the one you can only see
when I'm looking up?

Accent it.

# Something Better Than This Couch

Last January saw us cozy
on the couch, our pretzel
arms toasting by the fire.

A fresh-from-the-oven kind
of goodness filled the air
as we plunged into our corner
bakery treats. Warm blueberry
bagels. Coffee, no cream.

Your salty skin whet
a thirst for something.
Something like my tongue
tracing figure eights
across your brawny back.
Something like your body
trembling, not because
you're cold, but because
I've put you on the edge
of something better than
this couch. Something
better than the goodbye
coming from your mouth.

# Drowning Tides of Depression

My head hangs blue,
a buoy in rough seas.

Looking down
there's no way out.

Waves flood my mind,
persistent and intrusive.

    Creatures laugh at me . . . but why?

Shape-changing clouds morph
into soul-sucking man-eaters.

I grow horns.
It's the only way I know
to survive.

## The Wane of Your Existence

I threw your testicles to the clouds
and took a sip of the moon
the day you hopscotched out of my life.

It tasted like soy milk, the moon—
with chunks of bean curd
salt and acid, enzymes
to grind between my teeth,
make tofu out of you

subtlety, your come-
uppance, a corona
around my mouth.

# Cyclical Illusions

Flute
the earth
with narrow
arms. Watch grey roots
expand as wistful limbs span the sky,
a graceful ballerina arabesque
masked in sadness
swaying, wilting
gone.

## Consider Serenity

at three o'clock in the morning
when you somehow make it home,
barrel through the front door
grateful that you found your key

except you sense that something's off—
not the lights like they should be,
or the musky smell reminding you
to clean sometime soon,

but a fragrance not your own
that socks you in the face
like an overload of perfume
samples from department stores
you can't afford,

nearly knocks you to the floor
where you spy taupe Ropers,
but they're not yours
because you're wearing them,
and they're not his
because he doesn't like to two-step.

# Last Night

Red dust blew in
with condescending
compliments, left residue
on bedroom affections

that once belied the test of
nice-girl-meets-jerk-and-changes-him,

but the wind is a corkscrew
and weathercocks don't lie.

# Car Wash

Trapped
beneath an octopus blue,
outstretched arms
beat me
down
down
down
a smothering embrace.

I suffocate, palpitate
back and forth
the hours merely minutes
down
down
down
squeezing fear from each pore.

Until the tentacles rise
and I swim away.

# The Tempest

Her hair a rustle,
leaves of willows
dancing in the breeze

a mask to hide behind,
blinded by
piercing sheaths
of self-doubt.

Unbearable, this fervor
a predicament
she finds herself in
more times than not

like brittle bones,
bending charm
unpredictable,
never knowing when
she might snap.

# Running in Circles

Through tall timbers
I jounce, twist limbs—
a toilsome trail,
destination unknown.

I trip and fall
over knotted roots
protruding from the fallow ground
like knuckles fisted in my face,
a threatening trap.

I bounce, swallow dirt.
Pokes of pine needles
the reality checks
I ignore.

Hollow trunks echo
lies, lies, lies
putrefied, a rotten stump
with shallow appeal,

each lap
around the periphery
a step back.

# Gibbous Orbit

She sits on a moonbeam,
one leg to chest
the other dangling—
life's changing tides.

He sees around her
crescent silhouette,
an aureole against
oceanic waves.

He sees through
the umbrage
of her embrace,
celestial smiles
that lighten
with each orbit.

He sees beneath
abyssal eyes,
external lies
as vast as outer space,

the lines across
her flawless face
galactic.

# About the Moon

How many poems
have been written
about the moon?

About its opulence
in the funereal sky,
a petal in the wind

enchanting spells
cast upon oneiric
lovers in the night

ethereal complexities,
a beacon calling forth
the naysayers and doubters,

daring them to take a chance
on one more whisper in the dark

osculate the air,
taste it in the dewy grass
feel it in the atmosphere

while a widow lies awake
and looks to heaven,

pleading for permission
to move on.

# Another Chance

February scooted its way
through the revolving door
like a guilty dog, tail
drooping between hind legs.

It wasn't winter's gray veil
forming shadows of regret
that enduring six more weeks
of icicle hell creates,
the lack of sun a thief
depleting priceless moods

or that forgotten Valentine
all alone at the bar
downing Vodka shots
while couples everywhere
express their love.

No, it was you
calling me
from jail
begging for
another chance.

# Buried Alive

Engulfed, a lunge
of blinding dust
encumbers me. I
choke on swallowed
dreams while *you*

you kneel on narrow
hips of earth,
bow your shallow head
agnostically,
thrust pieces
of my heart
into the sky.

A secret silence
leaps through the air,
the stillness all around
a beat in time.

# What Happened on Texas Highway 105

Etched in my mind
your contorted face
and jaded eyes, unnerved

as the crisp autumn day
fades to dusk, and the sky
morphs into an inferno
of amaranth and heliotrope

as I shout, "Watch it!"

as you swerve the truck so fast
I slide across the seat into you

as the armadillo on the shoulder
transforms from arc to sphere

as you slam on the breaks,
push me away,

say you feel imprisoned,
my insecurities a whirling dervish
spurring a constant need to justify
every! single! thing! you! do!

say I *poke-poke-poke*
until you just give in.
I'm like a cactus,
soak you dry.

I don't want to be listening to you,
or feel the thumping of my chest

bass blaring, surround sound
honky-tonk blues.

I want to be that armadillo
with thick armor to protect me
from the hurt, the pain
you've caused again.

I roll into a ball
and close my eyes,
watch pieces of my heart
chip away.

# You, Skewered

Saturate me
with control,
your slight of words
when I cross the threshold
of your rolling expectations.

I might draw
a sword on you one day
when you're not looking,
skewer you with a finesse
as bold as your sigh,

watch you struggle
on your crooked back—
arms and legs
waving in the air
like a slimy cockroach
waiting to die.

# Locked In a Closet

Naivety blinds, ignorance deafens
sips turn to gulps turn to chugs
and you never know how you ended up
cornered in your porch closet
playing doorknob tug-of-war
with a stalker.

You lock yourself in, then want to die
for being so! fucking! stupid!
because a hairy pervert probably
sits on the couch waiting for you
to come through the sliding glass doors,

*a figure you thought the rising sun*
*mirrored in the pre-dawn window*
*until the rustling of leaves alerted you*
*from the bushes—up, up, up*
*over the balcony rail,*
*too fast to think about anything*
*before he arrived, so you pulled*
*the door shut, locked yourself in,*
*feeling his resistance.*

Fifteen minutes of he's-going-to-rape-me-
murder-me-what's-death-like-oh-my-God-
please-help-me emotions a bungee jump.
Time passes, but you don't know how long,
your cigarette forgotten in the coffee cup
where it floats. You sweat, clammy skin.
You can't stay locked in a closet forever.

Bravery is a fleeting thought,
with adrenaline made real.
You grab a hammer
from the red toolbox
your father gave you
when you left home
and finally gain
courage to open the door
where birds' morning songs
greet you, bacon sizzles
somewhere in the near distance
and the freeway comes to life
(you wonder why the hell you moved
so close to it)—all normal routines

while you obsess
about getting raped,
or tied up and tortured,
kidnapped . . . even dying;
but you slink forward anyway
like Clarice in *Silence of the Lambs*,
weapon in the air, ready to strike.
You hold your breath. One foot
in front of the other. S-l-o-w-l-y
slide open the door. Enter
your apartment.

Suddenly you're super-
woman in a robe, checking
corners and closets,
the bathtub, under
the bed, in the fridge

because if you're fast
enough, he just might
go away.

# While She Stayed in New Orleans

Blue couch spent a summer
in climate-controlled storage

along with the other furniture
crowding her empty heart.

They had a good time resting,
a much-needed  b r e a k

from the wear and tear of moving around.
They talked about her secrecy,

cried about what she did at night
when she thought no one was watching.

# A Cold Discovery

Knotted knee socks with worn holes in heels,
old faded argyles of grey and teal
*(the burgundy lacking symbiotic appeal)*

—s t r e t c h e d o u t—

yet warm for my feet, thought I'd try anyway
until *!clunk!* the diamond you gave me that day
*(before you admitted you were gay)* . . .

kerplunked from the toes,
a love gone astray now dredging up woes
*(I think I'll stick with anklets).*

# Mummified

Pine knots pop,
flames wave—
a ghoul
from beyond the grave.

Winter chills
fill the living room.
Your eyes entomb.

# Forgiving Scrutiny

I wince beneath
your lambent eyes
looking down upon me
like an adumbration,

a ghost that knows
my inner thoughts,
but does nothing
to acknowledge them.

Locked between our stare,
your silence mesmerizes me—
a maelstrom stalemate.

I know within
those sparkling flecks
of wheat and depths of gold,
is clemency,
but who am I to ask?

# Snowed

They say it's snowing somewhere
off in the distance, past the ocean's

    line  of  separation.

Up north where leaves of yellow, red, and orange
fill the black and white page with passion

and lined coats are more than closet fillers
soaking in the acrid smell of stale mothballs.

Yes, it's snowing where you are
while I seesaw on the cusp, indecision a

    line  of  separation.

The warm breeze drifting through my car
like the whisper of your voice.

# To Watch Someone Else Drinking Death

Once clear and blue, your eyes are eggs,
the whites covered in broken yolk,
scrambled with pain. There's no depth
within their blank fixation, only tears.
Tears running down dark recesses of obsession,
tears rolling down skin jaundiced and bruised,
into a retention pond that is you.
And you're killing yourself.

It is strong, this fatal disease.
It is a tapeworm in the soul
that eats away all inhibition, corroding
morals and values, sucking the life
out of self-esteem, hooking onto
egotistical monomania.

It is an old lover
in the middle of the night,
in the day, in good times and bad,
drooling at the mouth with lust
for one more taste, one more rendezvous.

> "*This time it'll be okay, this time you'll come
> with me into drunken ecstasy. I promise
> I won't hurt you this time.*"

It is a bully on the playground calling out names,
ridiculing every part of who you think you are.
It is a thief and a chronic liar digging a hole
in your aching heart, robbing you of love.

*"You're a loser, a worthless pile of shit.*
*I'm the only one who understands. You need me*
*to make it through the day. I'll cover up your fear.*
*Come on . . . drink me."*

And soon it fries your brain.
Like an egg.
Like your yellow eyes and skin.
Like your swollen liver.

Staunch denial is a heavy cloak smothering you
with immense cravings you can't allay by yourself.
I want to help, I really do; but I'm not God.

## Nowhere Else to Go

You run. You run and you run and you run, trying to free yourself from the pain, trying to stay sober a little longer each day. It's so hard. Your body cries out, but you keep running and running and running like Forrest Gump. You learn to evade all the viscous demons snapping at your feet. You trip and skin your knee, but you get back up. You want to go home, but have no idea where that is. You run and run . . . back to your childhood town, back to Mom and Dad.

# Selective Amnesia

Lasting scars
a child's knee
each with a story . . .

*falling, tripping*
*weaving, skipping*

black, purple, yellow, green,
the bruises of misery and pain

farther apart
the scabs /slash/ scars /slash/ hangovers

the THROBbing head
spinnING bed

*falling, tripping*
*weaving, skipping*

cotton /slash/ blood /slash/ in your mouth
a bitter taste of denial

until the next time.

## Acute Pancreatitis

That morning, when you opened the card I gave you, our laughter
launched distressing pain I thought merely a consequence of last night's
indulgence—lasagna and Scotch.

An hour later in church, you sat and stood and knelt while I
remained hunched over cradling my stomach like a sick child, hoping the
pressure might alleviate the pangs' lancination
through my mid-section.

After the service, I said I needed to go back to my apartment, drink chamo-
mile tea, rest awhile on the couch. I was in labor, waiting it out, contrac-
tions strong enough to blind, although I wasn't really pregnant and I'd
had no child, but I'd heard all the stories, and desperately wanted to be a
mother one day.

I watched *Apollo 13* on TV and tried to find a comfortable position; there
was no comfortable position. I closed my eyes and floated in space.

Dinner was at five, it was four. My stomach hurt so bad I couldn't stand
or sit, eat or drink. I called you, said I was sorry for ruining the party, but
I needed Dad to drive me to the hospital; someone had stabbed my abdo-
men with a knife, twisted it, dug deeper and deeper, butchering my intes-
tines, chopping them up all the way through to my back.

In the ER, they spun me around a table, flipped me upside-down like an
astronaut. I cried because it was Mother's Day.

# Stilling Spirits

Across the sofa, curtains drape—
a handkerchief to dry my tears
as in the pillows I escape
illusions laced and shattered years.
Manipulation of false fears
maudlin music, jaded eyes;
vast depths which drove a vault of shears—
avenged, I snapped and watched you die.

# Why You Have to Change People, Places, and Things

I watched him homebrew his own batch, a job
more refined than harvesting crops,

this friend I'd come to visit—
my old drinking buddy with fringe benefits

making brewski in front of my eyes,
something I'd never tasted from scratch.

I said I'd be fine, I'd walk the dog
while he went to play eighteen holes of golf

which I did briefly until around the block
voices in my head started lying to me

convincing me it would be different this time,
that just a sip would be okay. I rushed home

with the dog who wanted to stop every few
strides and chase squirrels up trees, until

at last suds like spume on the beach filled my mouth,
a perfumed delight (even though I wanted to puke)

the memories of a month ago embedded in my mind—
too late to go back, the craving a tidal wave.

## When She's Ready

It wasn't planned, each forward
step a downhill, backwards set-
back, the descent to hell
a whiskey sip away. She
failed to see the skid
marks in the street
or the puddles
by the curb
as death.

# When I Was a Worm

I dug a hole to China
in search of
William Shakespeare,

my self-worth
a shot of Tequila
in a never-ending well,

and I found myself
in the bottom of the pit,
swinging my legs
from the last
blade of grass,

rotting with each
passing breath.

# Rock Bottom

A new man popped into her life one fall,
a crutch to shape her squelched identity.

By November, they planned for a small
country wedding at the city park gazebo
with the high school choir to sing
and the Baptist preacher husband
of a teacher colleague to marry
(although she was Catholic
and her father refused to attend,
so her sister met with their priest
and they prayed for her all day).

A secret she kept hidden
from the country boy who lived
in a trailer, kept wild hog meat
in the fridge and piles of clothes
on the kitchen table,
but didn't drink.

The week of the wedding, a hidden
but not forgotten bottle of Vodka
called her to finish it off
(because she was sure she'd no longer
drink when she became a wife).

So she chugged through gags and chokes
to finish the liquor. When he picked
her up she fell in the parking lot,
bounced her chin off cars, then down
to the concrete where it split open
like pomegranate. The engagement ring

he bought from Sears but had yet to be sized
flew off her hand, landed somewhere in the bushes,
never to be seen again.

Like him.

# Fatalities

A cuss word, the C-word

death's inferno
igniting fear—

with the mere mention
of its name,
fumes of denial
smother immortality.

A word that must be spelled
with a whisper

   c-a-n-c-e-r

an omnipresence
disrupting peace,
burying futures
like Pompeii.

This C-word
that must be spelled
with a whisper

   c-a-n-c-e-r

slithers with a vengeance
shows its face
and yells, "I'm here!"
spits acrimonious venom

and progresses,

this chronic disease
of addiction, the A-word
as deadly as cancer—

    a-l-c-o-h-o-l-i-s-m.

# Why She Had a Problem with Religion

Schooled by nuns who stomped their feet
rapped knuckles with wooden rulers
condemned to hell individuality—

teenagers who stepped out of the box
with punked-up hair and body piercings
sent straight to the confessional

where horny priests drooled at the mouth
as they absolved them from all sin, said
to recite three Hail Marys and Our Fathers

in an empty church with perfect pews
lined up like rows of cabbage,
a stench of incense burning nerves.

# Questionings

Am I important enough to be heard?
How do I know God's will for me?
Does He live within and fill me with love?

How in the world can God hear me?
How can He listen to everyone's prayers?
Am I important enough to be heard?

Does He throw signs before my eyes?
Are angels disguised as friends?
How do I know God's will for me?

What is this overwhelming peace I feel?
Are God's whispers in my conscience reliable?
Does He live within me and fill me with love?

# Higher Power

They said
it could be
a tree,

Earth's telamon
with bark to rub my hands on
when I'm sweating a drink

a place to kneel
when burying
resentments

shade to help me
cool off
when irritable,

branches rustling me
into quiet meditation,

a strong, sturdy tree
like God.

# One Step at a Time

I.

while I sleep
a woodpecker drills
metal

II.

beneath the rubble—
silkworms await
enlightenment

III.

snowed in—
a cardinal appears
on the windowsill

IV.

ants
rounding up crumbs
on linoleum squares

V.

a head bows
in the church courtyard—
autumn winds lifting

VI.

ocean's PMS—
a jellyfish stings
unexpectedly


VII.

a lone man paddles
his handmade pirogue
down the street


VIII.

on the list—
yes/ maybe/ never
amends


IX.

piles of shit—
absolution in
puppy dog eyes


X.

road rage—
a car stops
for a turtle

XI.

emerging
a Monarch butterfly—
spring's covenant


XII.

after the storm
the tree stands firm—
communion

## Mental Obsession

I decided
to make it irritating
when I really should have
ignored the gurgling sound
that grated on my nerves;
blowing bubbles from a straw.
Over and over, the vibration
making raspberries with taut lips
breathing life into the backwash
of your gin and tonic:
I know you're drunk again
but I'm not
so stop.

# Jonesing

He carries cigarette butts on his shoes
secured beneath dirty laces,
ready to grab in a split second
if that's all he has—
a second—
to run outside and puff
maybe once, maybe twice,
but he'll save it for later
and that's okay—
he's been clean a week now.

# While Waiting for a Table at the Bar

Solicitude eludes you, but I
shudder at the thought
of      one      more      drink.

A brick-house waitress
shoulders cocktails,
her trail intoxicates

     . . . whiskey teasing . . .
     . . . vodka taunting . . .

me to feel different
from this unknown now.

Wisps of cigarette smoke
drift through the air
with arms that WaVe

    *come here, come have just one*
    *sip of alcohol*
    *. . . this-time-it-will-be-okay . . .*

Your vacant eyes follow
the brick part of the waitress, and I
wonder if you're thirsting for some-
thing other than a drink.

We order coffee straight up,
talk about the inky days
stored within our memories
the fuzzy stains of regrets,
sober now and filled with endless time.

It's awkward at first,
this blank space.

I fold my white napkin into triangles,
see how small they can get, while you
tap rhythms on the bar with your thumbs
-ba-da-ba-da-bump-bump-tap-tap- (sigh).

# Part II

# Upon the Blue Couch

Maybe I didn't write a thing today.
Maybe I sat on this twenty-year-old
muted blue couch and did nothing
but think about the wear and tear
from move after move we've been through,
with washed over mars, the scars
of cigarettes and vomit,
having been passed out upon and puked upon,
a shoulder when I needed one
to cry my eyes out upon.
Maybe I remembered all the lovers
who have lied
sprawled upon its pillows
with hungry lips I've kissed,
hands upon thighs, breasts upon chest,
all to feel something better than
what was missing in my heart.
Maybe I dreamed about my husband
and all the times we've rued upon
blue obsequious fabric,
worrying about the economy we've fallen upon—
with curse words or whispers
sometimes at opposite ends,
sometimes hand in hand,
but always with a love
never to be crashed upon.
Maybe I recalled my babies
sleeping upon their daddy
sleeping upon the cushions
as they sought solace in colicky times
and I was too tired to stay awake,
my nipples having been sucked upon

and sipped upon one too many times,
their cracks a small sacrifice
for a lifetime of nourishment.
Maybe I didn't write a thing today,
but this twenty-year-old blue couch did.

# I Feel Your Presence

Sometimes
goose bumps wave through my body
like leaves that rustle in a sudden wind,
or a rapid burst of thrill during a parade
when I feel the drums beat within,
hurl insistent pressure from my heart
unfurl a spasm of peace.
I feel your presence.
It's no enigma, this sense of love
nor rare, if I remain keenly aware.
My fists unclench, the walls around me fall
as a sensation spacious and freeing,
an overwhelming feeling orgasmic,
crashes down all my insecurities
once devastating, now nothing
compared to you.
I feel your presence.

# His Poem

He once wrote a poem for me
about the wind and the waves,
how the ocean breeze felt upon his face
breathing in the salty air
as water lapped upon his feet
in rhythmic solitude
a moonlit night, a starry sky
sitting on the wooden pier
two hearts as one.
Nothing could compare, he wrote
and sent it with a card,
the poem I keep beside our bed.

# When You Didn't Want to Wake Me

My eyes opened
to emptiness,
the usual indention
from your head
missing.
Had work called you
out in the middle
of the night again?
I stumbled
to the kitchen,
turned on
the coffee pot,
passed the couch
in semi-darkness
to the phone,
cursing your job
as I dialed your pager

nearly jumped
to the ceiling
at the first buzz,
a vibration
from behind.

"What the heck?"
two voices
at the same time—
yours and mine.
"I just got home.
Don't they know
I need some sleep,"
you said, then turned
around and looked at me.

I laughed alone.

# I Married a Marine

When we met, he was skinny
and had a buzz cut.
I told him he looked
like a prisoner of war
with muscles, emaciated
but still a hunk.

When he became a father
he stopped shaving.
Soon a bushy mustache
went with the head of hair
he'd grown out for our wedding.
I told him he looked
like a movie star,
only tired.

When it morphed into
a woolly bear caterpillar
sitting below his nose,
I wouldn't kiss him.

When I mentioned *armyworm,*
he immediately
started back with the buzz cuts,
got rid of the hirsute lip.

I told him he looked
much better that way,
like a Marine.

# Advancements

They make chains now
that stay put

no slips or slides
to the front or back sides,
no clasps to be seen
dangled or jangled
at the nape of my neck

just lush lips to kiss,
tonguing your way down
my quivering
chest.

# Marriage Changes Everything

When you went to Japan,
I drove you to the airport
two hours away
at midnight,
wondered how I'd survive
ten days without you.

When you went to Greece,
you drove yourself
to the same airport
while I headed straight
to the post office

applied for a passport,
my picture a blank stare.
That night, the kids and I
brought a puppy home.

# When Baby Comes Along

You talk of fizzy bath bombs
with bottles of champagne.

>Well, I think you're crazy
>to think of such things.

The babe needs my breast,
blurs my chesty mind

>and the last bath I've had
>was the quick washout kind.

So take your fizz bubbles,
get buzzed by yourself

>while I daydream of saunas
>with my own bookshelf.

# Phone Conversation with an OB/GYN Nurse

I'm miserable.

        Have you lost interest in things you used to enjoy?

*Well, duh. I've had three kids in four years.*
All I do is sit on the couch and nurse.
I don't have time for anything else.

        Do you find it hard to get out of the bed in the morning?

*Well, duh. I've had three kids in four years.*
*What's your problem, woman?*
I never get any sleep.

        Do you find it hard to concentrate?

*Well, duh.*
Huh? Oh, when I have time to take a shower,
sometimes I forget if I've shampooed my hair
or soaped my body. Is this normal?

        Are you irritable?
        How's your appetite?
        What about your sex drive?

*(Babies screaming so loud, I can't hear)*
**WHAT DID YOU SAY?**

        **Are you irritable?**
        **How's your appetite?**
        **What about your sex drive?**

Didn't you hear me? I nurse, so I eat!
I don't sleep because I nurse!
Sex has not been a problem;
I've had three kids in four years!
I don't think I use soap!
So, yes, sex is not fun.
Forget I ever called!

*Slam. Sniff, sniff.*

## Everlasting Cord

Eclipsed—
my mind, body, spirit,
one with you.

I held tight your hand
after the separation,
a cord extending forever

sometimes with too much slack,
sometimes like a tightrope.

Always, always not far away,
and ready to reel you in.

# Helpless Victims of a Distracted Driver

One moment in June,
our life changed.
A call with words
hardly heard,
screams and shouts—
*He hit us! Get here fast!*
Our car, an accordion
with a monster truck
untouched.
On the corner,
a teen shouting
*I'm sorry!*
His confession—
a change
of radio stations,
eyes off the road,
rear end unknown.
*You hit my family!*
A scream from me.
My baby crying
hysterically—
where were
the other two?
Lemonade
in the house
across the street,
a friend,
how nice.
An ambulance
hours waiting,
the older kids okay.

That night,
sitting on the couch,
picking shards of glass
from baby's head,
husband crying out
in pain.

# Giving UP

I watched the twin towers
fall while nursing,
didn't turn off the news
until Christmas.
The instant replays
sucked me dry
as hormonal imbalance
began to bare
its grisly teeth.
Cold cabbage leaves
helped alleviate the pain
in my hardened breasts.
I wished I could place them
on my heart.

When Katrina hit,
I cried with
Anderson Cooper,
then found myself
volunteering
at the Salvation Army
organizing clothes and food,

unaware that
less than a month later
Rita would unsettle me,
evacuating the family
with millions of people
out for a Sunday drive,

and that after
nearly ten years,
I'd say screw it
and put the bottle
to my mouth again

while someone's
only shelter,
a tent,
blew out to sea.

# Thirty Days

A tugboat rattled her from sleep,
foghorns blowing louder each time.

Her head pounded to the beat,
or was it a freight train
vibrating the single bed?

Why was she sleeping
in her clothes,
a thirsty sponge?

Snoring, someone snoring—
three cacophonous rasps of breath
followed by a long pause
of nothing, nothing.
What happened?
Certainly, not death.

Out of bed, a rush
across the room
closer, closer, hand
reaching for pulse

and then a sudden
loud snore explosion

hurry back to bed
knees to chest,
tumbling heart
scare.

How would she endure thirty days of this?

# Redirected

seeking answers
in gray clouds,
a cardinal
chirps from telephone wire
and catches my eye

# Sidereal Stars in First Love Eyes

What better time than now—

    as the cool wind rustles your golden
    locks and leaves dance through the air,
    as the blue sky as clear as your skin
    fills the autumn day with transparency

to tell you *V* stands for values,
and just because the birds venture
north each winter, return in the spring,
it doesn't mean your heartthrob will
return or change or tell you he loves you
for any reason other than he wants to
score a victory for his flock of peers.

What better time than now—

    as you sway with branches, reach
    the stars sparkling in your hazel
    eyes, and your fingers fly off
    the keys, texts faster than jets

to tell you how deep emotions drift
like clouds, change as fast as they
cover the sun, turn a moment from
bright to grey; and can fool you
into thinking first love
is heaven, when it's
really just another
thunderstorm
waiting
to strike.

## Naming Weapons

He said he'd name it "Discipline"
whatever the weapon might be—
a sword or bow and arrow,

imagination heightened
as he ran through the house
warding off his brother
with kicks and jabs
undisciplined.

Blown, the injustice of stature
marked in slices of pepperoni pizza
and Harry Potter accents—

because it's all about control, he says.

Not the gun that goes off somewhere
in the middle of the night,
an elderly man killing an intruder,
only it was his wife.

Name that "Careless".

# How to Climb a Rope

They watched you mount
the rope and start to climb
(once a Marine, always a Marine)
our kids so proud, with jaws
dropped in awe, hands
sheltering wide eyes
from the autumn sun.

Your body (still as lean
and tone as the day we met)
haunted me with each cross-
ankled lift and side-saddled
shift, the rope between your
legs a squeeze between my
thighs, a taunting lure, this
allure, a stir of yearning
for your prowess.

You jumped down, asked us
what we thought. The boys,
a miniYOU, and our daughter,
so beautiful sometimes you cry,
not one to miss an honest dare
(I wonder where they got that from)
swore to do the same that day and I,
with hands a fan across my face,
said it was too hot to stay outside.

Your countenance a glimpse of dawn
as you followed me.

# My Awful-izing Mind

I know you're working
in the double-bottom ballast tanks,
a place lower than low;
so low the air is a vacuum,
so low filth fills every orifice on your body,
so low I taste it when I kiss you hello,
so low there's no reception
for your cell.
You've been there for hours,
in this tanker of a ship
in a town an hour away,
longer than I think safe—
and I can't reach you.
The news comes on, there's been a wreck
on the highway known for killer wrecks—
the highway under construction
with narrow lanes and piles of cars,
the highway you must take home;
a given bottleneck with no recourse
and you're not here.
You should be home by now.
I dial your number, no answer.
I call and call and call.
My mind has reached the pit,
lower than a mind should go,
thinking things a mind like mine
shouldn't think about.
You're hurt in the bottom of the ship
all alone without your cell.
You're trapped inside your car,
demolished by the eighteen wheeler.
All the sudden I'm crying.

How will I live without you?
How will I tell the kids?
How will we survive?
The funeral was a nice affair,
the one I'm ruing over when I get the call;
you'll be home soon. Not soon enough.

# Advice on Chaperoning Middle School Boys for Out-of-Town School Weekend Event

Don't sleep, or even plan to
unless you have earplugs
or sleeping pills,
which you'd better cut in half
or you'll never wake up in the morning

to find toothpaste spit
all over the mirror and sink, handle and counter
with rubber bands from braces everywhere
and water from the shower on the floor
toilet seats UP (so look before you sit)

cookie crumbs in bed, drink spills
farts like stink-bomb missiles
giggles, snorts, jokes
dirty clothes everywhere
lamps unplugged for electronics charging
attempts at watching forbidden shows
whispers . . .

Did I mention pills?
Maybe you should take Prozac.

# Spousal Communication and Forgetfulness

The father of that toddler-with-a-head-full-of-red-curls-like-a-wet-mop-in-
diapers-who-got-stuck-in-our-dog-kennel

called. You know, the one I went to school with
who married a Pilates instructor?

It was the birthday party where we set up
that mammoth water slide in the backyard,
the one we borrowed from . . . oh, my friend
whose husband is a professional baseball player,
and you spent days patching up holes,

but during the party, it started
raining, so everyone dashed
into the house soaking wet

and we didn't have a plan B,
only pizza and lots of boys,
but learned real quick we
always needed to have a plan B

or else toddlers might back themselves
into mysterious places to escape pandemonium.

You know, they live
in that two-story-house-with-green-shutters
on the street that what's-her-name lives on?

Yes, him!
He wanted to know
if we had room
for another dog.

# Us, Captured

As drizzle turns to sleet and sheets the windows white.

As crackling embers knot winter's chill, a pop of firecrackers from afar.

As hazy warmth spreads across the hearth to where I sit, my heart a blanket of desire.

As my eyes look down upon your hands holding mine, a grasp that through the years has grown in strength.

As all distress melts into pools of candle wax, and muffled breaths turn to longing sighs.

As this moment in time is captured like a single snowflake on an eager tongue.

As you are, I am; here.

# No Need for Smiles

Opaque expression
cuts the bleak atmosphere
with desolation, my breath
a touch of misery.

At least that's what you think,
your nebulous assumption
based on my demeanor,

but I'm at peace—
no longer do I feel the need
to flash red-carpet smiles,
pretend that I'm happy
when I'm just okay,
or not.

My heart is a torch
blazing with love.
If you hover long enough
you'll sense a tender touch,

a vision clear as water
might wash over you,
inner contentment
might flow inward out

so that when I do smile
you'll know it's real.

# Reverse Aging

You get to the age when
*it won't happen to me*
happens to you,

and once the shock wears off
you realize life as you know it
will never be the same.

Cymbals clash and still
you drive in reverse
where young adulthood
is an open field,
a place you jog in bare feet
without pain crashing through
aging joints                    and the only fork

is something between your fingers
stabbing steamy baked potatoes
loaded with sharp cheddar cheese
oozing out the side, a stick of butter
sour cream, bacon, chives

and mixing it all together
instead of grilled chicken,
peas and brown rice.

# When the Doctor Said Three Words

Blood rushed through my veins
like a turbulent river,
and I was on a tube
riding the rapids.
You were close behind,
our arms entwined
until a sudden surge
swept me away.

I was engulfed in water—
swallowing it
breathing it
blinded by it
hearing . . . that roar.

You tried to catch me.
I shouted out
until all
I heard
was . . . nothing

but the doctor saying,
*perhaps a tumor.*

# MRI: Memory Recalling Instruments

Held for ransom, sucked into a barrel.
The only demand—complete stillness,
not! even! a crinkle! of the nose!
For peace of mind, freedom from pain
it's worth it. I navigate ahead,
withstand the cacophonous irritation.

  *Rump-a-pum-pum.*

Adagio . . . allegro, little drummer boy . . .
I'm at Mardi Gras and the marching band nears.
My heart beats to the rhythm of the drums.

  *Clickety-click-click-clack.*

Tapping across the stage in unison
hair gathered in taut bun, little part on left
bright red lips, big smile. What a show!
Recital's right around the corner.

  *Silence. Breathe.*

Dear God,
Please stay with me
send some of those warming vibes my way.

  *Pow! Pow! Pow!*

M-a-c-h-i-n-e guns from all angles—
I didn't mean that, God.

  HONK! HONK! HONK!

An alarm. Thieves running out the department store.
At least they didn't shit in the dressing room,
too many clothes to hang up, why'd I agree
to work in the Juniors section?

Cha-ching!

I'd much rather be at The Chicken.

# Goggled

I'm diving in
   blind,
      barely breathing
while someone waves a fish in the air.

My palms
   come together
      in prayer
then fan out, drawing hearts in the water.

I kick
   without a splash,
      swim away from middle age,
         away from this Botox brochure
           skewing my field of vision.

# Speaking With Eyes

They sat holding hands,
her walker within reach—
the years behind them written
in their countenance.

They drifted in and out of sleep,
their nodding heads in sync, or so it seemed
until someone slammed the bathroom door.

Our eyes then met,
hers said it was horrible—
and I wondered if she meant
the colonoscopy or diagnosis.

Mine said I understood
as my husband's name was called,
and together we walked back
to hear the news.

# On Receiving the Diagnosis of Crohn's Disease

*Crohn?* The only *Kron* I'd
ever known was Russell,
an unassuming
never-stirs-up-trouble
kinda guy.

Perhaps they meant
*crone?* A warty witch
casting evil spells
in her cauldron,

dumping acid and bile
that churn your stomach
with each whir, pouring
poison down your throat,
a raspy coat
straight
to your ass
that seethes and bleeds
each time
a gassy morsel
won't dissolve,

taunts the night
with sweats and chills, cramps
unexplainable pain,
unrest, a protest, this stomach up-
set we once thought drainage
but . . .

that's it—
a Teenage Mutant Ninja Turtle
*clone*, not *crone,* an evil *clone*
living in the sewer
distilling noxious fumes
through pipes, depriving
you of a normal life,
this curse invading you
in the gut—a stab, a twist
of Crohn.

## Curved-Mirror Effigy

Scattered daydreams
like mist on glass,

straw strewn upon the edge
of amber fields

a whiffle in the wind
drawing eyes to stop and rest.

At center, a windmill
with rusty blades hypnotic

squeaks in revolution
a lullaby.

# Prestigious Mockery

I want to scream—
grab my knotted hair, pull
its teabag roots and run.

    Then I want to stop—
    a disillusioned child
    with Cinderella dreams.

Austere in light—
a contrast, palpable;
as murky as the shadows
on this house.

    Time—a chiseled bone—
    mocks contentment
    in seedy shades
    of prestige.

Shelved, the pain—
an imminent cloud
that like an arctic front
blows lines across the sky

in these signs of squalid time.

# When a Dove Nearly Hit the Car

{Wispy wings}
caressed the windshield,
s~w~o~o~s~h of feathers
like waltzing willow leaves
as delicate as a baby's touch
with downy skin
to finger stroke, up and down
a silken face, bleary eyes
opened just enough to see
the spirit shine inward»out,
swathed—eternal love.

{Wispy wings}
ballerina arms, elegance
as gorgeous as a mourning dove
arabesque, a pose of grace
a spinning pirouette
spinning away
a skirr in the endless sky
growing smaller with each beat—
too far to reach,
too far gone,
like you.

# Hunkering Down

Our box of important papers is in the backseat with the dogs. I hurry into the house. Grab milk, eggs, bacon. Everything else might get ruined if the electricity goes out, but there's no room at my parent's house for all of our food. I remind everyone to buckle up. Off-beat clicks, swishing windshield wipers. Three minutes later, we are in Mom and Dad's driveway unloading suitcases and toys. When I walk inside, the Weather Channel is tracking Ike's path. I head to my old room. Dump stuffed animals on floral quilt. My old sunshine comforter sits on closet shelf. I run down the stairs. Back up and down again like I used to. Five times. I'm winded, but feel better. The kids devour homemade chocolate chip cookies. Later on they want to play *Life*.

> hurricane season—
> an empty birdhouse knocks
> against the awning

# Plea to Hoarder with Blue Tarp on Roof Seven Years

Blue hangs over your head
follows you around,
a tattered tarp
with wings flapping
hollow wind.

Musty madness,
this useless junk
stacked against
the border of your heart

yesterday's headlines,
a time when the world
complied to your desires,
now collecting dust, mental
obsessions the possessions
you refuse to abandon.

Covered with the blues,
your life hovers—
a gargoyle calling out
to all who cross your path
for seven odd years now
a gaudy eyesore,
your decrepit façade,
falling apart like it did
when Rita blew through.

Tell me, how much longer
until tawdry melancholy
diminishes to nothing
but a sun-bleached scar,
abandoning all hope
for neighborly accord?

# Swamp Things and Poetry

Parallels and verticals criss-cross
across the swamp, gnarled cypress
trees convert Spanish moss into covens
of humped-over witches with warts and
crooked noses, trunk stumps the stools
they sit upon. Emerald algae auras
in the smog reflect evil grins, wicked
cackles mere wayward croaks as frogs
leap pad to pad; this obstacle course
where swaying grey chokes ideas. Cobwebs
cobble wrinkles in your mind, wrestle with
incoherent words until you swallow whole
what you thought the weakest link, but
in actuality wrests poetic wizardry.

## Bidding Farewell

Bye-bye April
with your wishy-washy ways,
windy stream of consciousness
fickle as a falling leaf

the days of hot and cold,
a topsy-turvy hint of spring
the glint of sunshine promises
wisped away, adversity

like words remixed, poetry
raining down upon my psyche
hopping like a rabbit, teasing
games of hide-n-seek—
catch me if you can.

Down the hole
expanded depths
Utopia, it seems
casting out all fear
of time consumed.

# Costly Repercussions

Shamed, in this uncomfortable
comfortable chair as you work on me
like a welder, say the enamel's all gone,
but at least my gums are healthy.

I wonder what you really think
when I open my mouth. It tells
the story of despair, ancient ruins
journaled through time.

I talk to you, you talk to me
but no words come out, only thoughts
resounding through the high-pitched drill.

I beg for your understanding, say I wish
I'd listened all those years ago, heeded
the warnings I thought for someone else.

I was too self-absorbed, eternally unique,
my arms wrapped around the little secret
I kept hidden in the bosom of control,
striving for approval.

It's been twenty years now,
but I'm still suffering
the consequences
of past imprisonment,
my collateral a high-priced mouth—
titanium, porcelain, root canals, crowns
with front teeth worn too thin to last twenty more.

# Burial

My tooth died today.
I buried it in the backyard
with all the other teeth
killed by decay,
wrapped it in a red velvet
ring box, snapped it shut tight.

    Under the oak tree
    where I once carved your name,
    now only bones remain.

I traded it for porcelain
and a titanium rod, the hollow roots
filled with thousands of dollars
of regret.

# Plant Factory

The air you breathe, unfiltered
filled with gasps of waste,
exhausted gas, a grasp
for something fresher
than what's here.

Sometimes a whiff
as rank as rotten eggs
stops me in my tracks, a drift
from miles away, coastal
wind a constant reminder
that the paper mill still floats.

You bear this stagnancy,
say you love the atmosphere
close to beaches, lakes, and woods
where you can clear your mind

but what about your lungs,
what about the trees?

# Politicking with a Lobster

I talked to a lobster last night,

    tried to tell it how fed up
    I was about the politics
    in my hometown,

    the complaining, the bitchery
    constantly nitpicking the cards
    they've been dealt, a race
    to an unmarked finish line

    the scandalous piranhas
    diving on chalkboards,
    inhaling words and numbers
    before the truth comes out

    the prestigious glory-seekers
    too damn set in their ways
    to adjust the budget,

    and with greed enough
    to fill an ocean

but the lobster turned bright red,
snapped me to pieces until I shut up.

# Part III

# Drinking Dreams

Night vision a blur,
a vertical illusion
taunting me, crying out
in stark delusion,
a haunting world
of prying schemes.

Imprisoned by
vivid images
of yesterday,
when supple lips
suckled Vodka,
latched on
to tainted sips
of dark oblivion,
the pain forgotten.

Reality
but a touch away,
a shake awake;
the nightmare realized.

# That Easter Weekend

We sat side by side that Good Friday,
shared our weekend plans;

you a date
with your husband,

and me preparing
for Easter.

On Saturday morning,

you put wine
in your purse
at the gas station

while I dyed eggs
with my kids.

At noon, I tried
to call you, worried
for reasons yet unknown

while you shot yourself
in the chest.

On Sunday,
I woke up
still crying.

# Bits and Pieces of Truth in the Night

Sleep felt as unreachable as the stars,
stars that refused to shine
while I prayed for the candlelight aura
to appear when I closed my eyes.

I wandered to the comfort of my blue couch,
the one that had supported me through years
and years of highs and lows, wear and tear
the springs' buoyancy always therapeutic,
but I'd never dealt with anything
like the depth of suicide
or the unanswered questions now sinking me.

A mystery, why you'd shoot
yourself in a heated moment like you did,
missing pieces I needed to find.
Alcohol. A fight. A neighbor's gun.
What about the night before?
The gap in time you spent with him,
a vacant hole of doubt.

I hoped to feel God's warm embrace
as I had so many nights before.
Instead you gave me a disco ball—
reds and purples, blacks and blues—
swirling in a kaleidoscope of confusion,
random flashes of what seemed to me as bodies.
A violent message I couldn't understand,
clueless as I'd ever been since you'd left,
empty as a cushion full of holes
on a couch with rusty springs.

# After She Found Out Her Roommate Had a Gun

A door in the wall
roused her from sleep
boundless shadows,
an eerie chill.

SLAM.

"You don't belong here."

Raspy words
at the retreat house
where she went
to clear her head.

She opened her eyes
to the barrel of a gun
an arm's length away

her drumming chest,
an explosion within.

"You don't belong here."

Was she screaming,
or had the gun fired?
Was she sweating,
or could it be blood?

## Space Invader Nadir

Drifting          a chasm

of inhumanity   l o s t

        in    a          mindless          void.

The only way                lifting

    the window of

                    c l o s e d - m i n d e d n e s s - -

how to get there,          a mystery.

    Confusion, the dead weight of egomaniacs

    riding on the backs of asteroids, flying

    through black holes alone.


Are we disillusioned - - - Martians,

falling
prey

        to insanity?

Or are they from - - - - outer space,

attempting to inhabit the earth?

# Haunted by the Past

What is this cadre in my mind
that misconstrues the images I see—
me, a mess, and you unharnessed?

A simulacrum amiss, identity
lost through acuity oblique.

Lies scream at me from within,
deceive my conscience, send
warped-reflection nightmares
I see as real, but in reality
you're my sentinel, emanating
mirthful confidence, trust—
a love unconditional and true.

On the steamy bathroom mirror,
I'm framed within your heart
yet I still see me
as a mere reflection
of a poor pathetic soul,
a parasite unwilling
to let go of illusory delusions
from another life
that haunt me still today.
But I'm working on it.

# Voiced

Poetry is . . .
the voice I'm scared to speak
unleashed in ways mystique
birthing words I need to hear,
that through past years of fear
formed a

~throttlehold~

and robotically, I molded
into silence.

Poetry is . . .
the strip I dare to tease
for whom I aim to please
in seductive, nasty ways
and with language quite risqué.

If the mood knocks at my door, I might
use words like *fuck* or *whore* in my piece
and it will be the best I've ever had
in this quest for poetry.

# Serenity

I always knew
there was a middle
because I'd seen it
swinging by.

It wasn't the hanging
by a thread
of false eyelashes
during recital,

or the sudden call back
to the floor
when the muffle
of Velcro is heard
in a silent gym,
a strip of
sparring gear

or the cough medicine's
dried-up drips
making sticky rings
in the cabinet,

or the vanilla coffee
aftertaste no
mouthwash can remove.

No, it was the ground
you walked on
while carrying me,
and the freedom felt
when I let you.

# Poetic Danseuse

Extrapolate clichés . . .
entice the mind with verbs pristine
resplendent as a prima ballerina,
entrechat across the silent stage.

From the mezzanine, a feat enchanting
an allure enticing watchful eyes
with sequins amaranth, azure
celestial bodies—poems alive.

## Playing Solitaire

Anchoretic accolades in a crowd,
the only sound a prayer,
a whisper here or there.
Merited—impromptu spasms;
clapping hands, whistling

still . . . in silence,
the fear a misstep
in my mind of never good enough
perception skewed, self-image

a drab and pesky squirrel
darting across the parapet,
hurry, hurry to the other side
before someone sees me screw up.

Except for you—I know you are here
with me always, ready to carry me
away from this corner shadow
where I sit quite and lonely,
but never NEVER alone.

# Carried by the Wind

Like a flap of Eagle's wings
or clash of tortuous seas,
the American flag
flies at half-mast.

While limbs are lost
and lives unfurled,
spring's wind revolts

reminds me that
no matter what,
tomorrow will come

even though at times
the world seems
upside down.

# What Is Beauty?

Nothing.
No sibling rivalry-snap-back-and-forth tug-of-war Armageddon.
No TV blaring in my ear, the only sounds I hear the constant bleeps of
curse words.
No old and cranky washing machine sounding possessed when the agitator
comes out during the spin cycle and nearly gives everyone a heart attack as
it rocks and knocks.
No dryer whirring, constant worry, whether or not the heat element will
work this time, if I'll have to hang the clothes to dry.
No dishwasher to unload—a clank of everyday dishes, silverware as the
kids put them away.
No worries yet about what's ahead, the children or husband;
what to cook, or not. God, I wish he liked chicken.

Just morning.
When I'm the only one awake as nature comes to life
sitting beside the window and drinking my first cup of coffee.
Listening to nothing but the birds' capriccio.
Spotting my cardinal on the wrought-iron plant stand.
Everything beautiful; nothing.

# Peace, Love, God, and Disco Balls

A disco globe spins
prisms in the theater—
play that funky music
and I'll transport you
back to a time of peace.

A time of love, hippies
tripping over John Lennon
smoking weed on the lawn
beads swinging in entryways
psychedelic colors, incense.

While today we walk around
like soldiers on land mines
tiptoe through department stores
stare at front doors as if borders
avoid eye contact with strangers
prepared to withdraw and hide
in a moment's flash.

We hold tighter to our babies
send our kids off to school in angst
aware of bullies and misbehavior,
cheaters, liars, thieves.

Inconsequential consequences
because there are none anymore,
just more, more, more—

    *I'll buy you more!*
    *Shut up, here it is—*
    *Cram this iPad in your mouth*
    *and leave me alone!*

No, we prepare our beloved children—
precious gifts we have been given—
for the possibility of peers
pulling guns out and shooting
—bam! bam! you're dead!—
for no other reason than they can. They can.

Anybody and everybody can
shoot dead the one who pisses them off,
the one who says no, sets boundaries
in this materialistic world

where God has become unimportant—
a misnomer, an old wives tale
a source of offense for nonbelievers
preaching freedom to deny His existence:
Take down the Ten Commandments!
Do away with prayer in school!

I watch the nation crumble
like an ant pile dIStuRbed,
a red-hot flurry seeking *what?*
In this "land of opportunity"
once coveted world-wide
now falling apart,

not from global warming
or doomsday predictions,
alien takeovers, UFOs,

but because something's missing
in our lives: peace, love . . . God.
And disco balls.

# Part IV

# Lack of Oxygen

On the phone
I notice it most,
your gasp for breath
a winded goodbye

like a child who holds
the phone too close,

or a speed walker
with one hand to ear,
talking to the air

before
the final
lap.

# I'm a Wreck

The wind spins my hair
into a mossy mess . . .
but I don't care.

My feet are stuffed
in knee high hose
that I dug up
from years ago . . .
but I don't care.

I pass Dr. Who
who's on the phone,
and Nurse Ratched
ratchets through
the elevator doors . . .
but I don't care.

I enter your meat
locker room
kiss your cheek,
your skin as cold
as ice sheets
but when you say
you're hotter
than hell . . .
well, I care.

# Long-Term Stay

An aquarium, the wall
greets eyes and pacifies
when elevator doors open,
but there's not much to explore
on the sixth floor—
your room on one end of the hall,
physical therapy on the other.

Midpoint, the nurse's station
is abuzz—too much paper work,
documentation gluing nurses
to chairs while impatient
patients call.

Opposite, a place
for occupational therapy—
a kitchen, conference table
with jigsaw puzzles, books.
In the corner, a couch and TV
for family to wait, fuel up
on weak coffee and cookies.

Somewhere in-between
is the secret laundry room,
a closet where I washed your hair.
The wheelchair leaned back
so your neck could rest
in the beauty shop-like sink.

What a fiasco, water
spraying the shiny floor,
my aim haphazard, our laughter
worth the hassle of backing
you into that shoebox space.

# A Saved Voice Message

You know the feeling
when you finally hear a loved one's voice
after the walls just caved in
for some reason or another
and you needed to hear their voice.
The tears come pouring out
and you choke and you snort,
your nose a water tap.
Because nothing matters except that voice.
Not the nagging you griped about for years.
Or the childhood resentments staining your heart.
Not the meddling into business you thought your own.
But the understanding that time is limited.
And you wish you could go back and do it all again
without pressing delete.

# When People Heard the News

Dad's golfing buddy offered you
Lourdes holy water from southern France,
made you drink it even though
you won't drink communal wine
your fear of germs too strong.

An acquaintance shared a sacred relic,
white cloth from the wooden cross of Jesus,
cloth that when touched or brushed upon the sick
performs miracles. So I rubbed it on your skin—
that seemed to have aged ten-fold in two weeks—
and hoped for a biblical phenomenon.

A prayer square gifted
by a Christian friend of a friend
that prayed for her when she needed it
and here she is to pass it on
to me to give to you.

Another said asparagus cures cancer, purée
in the morning and night, cold or hot,
with water or not, won't you try it?
Homemade chicken noodle soup
eating raw, certain herbs
drinking aloe
acupuncture
hypnosis
massage
tai chi
yoga

but after a while
we just hope
for a quick death.

# Chilled

Your room a morgue, I didn't mean to say,
although it's freezing in here.
I layer my clothes, yet I'm cold each day,
your room a morgue. I didn't mean to say
that, between teeth chattering away—
I'll likely survive another year.
Your room a morgue, I didn't mean to say,
although it's freezing in here.

# The Styrofoam Cup

limited: caffeine intake
from this Styrofoam cup
where the last gulp is my second
and the first a wake-up

call, aggressive
when you're down all night
trying to get comfortable
in that cold bed of white

noise, I'm a fetus
trying to stay warm
with heightened awareness
each move an alarm

clock, sleep's a dream
weak coffee, last hope
as sterile as this room
a Styrofoam cup

## Selective Disturbances

The elderly man
    catty-cornered from you
        calls out

        ~help me~

        his voice a ghost
        growing louder
        with each wale.

Add to that, a *tink*
of flatware against bedrail.

        ~help me, *tink*, *tink*~

        Panic echoes
        through the walls.

I watch you sleep
so sound, I fear
your chest too still

        ~help me, *tink*, *tink*~

but the draft beneath your nose
reassures me, your breath

like a balloon
bluer than your lips
when you just can't
tie it quick enough

and it flies
from your fingers,
crosses the room, then
falls to the floor,

deflated.

~help me, *tink, tink*~

# Temporarily (ab)Normal

It's like watching TV with my kids
and an ad comes on
for erectile dysfunction
or intimate lubricants—
*guaranteed arousal when applied*—
suggestiveness an awkwardness
driving me to change channels
or send the kids outside.

Only it's you
and the ads involve the holidays,
revolve around mobility and cheer
colors of the season, reds and greens
as matriarchs like you smile
over green bean casserole and corn
serve turkey on Corning Ware trays

while you lie coughing,
your oxygen tank          off
in the corner, a scolded child

and I sit beside you
watching the Macy's parade.

# An Epiphany

A messenger bird visited me today.
He neared from nowhere and landed
on my shoulder. I wondered what he
was doing here, why he didn't fly
off when I looked his way. Instead,
I heard a whisper urging me to let
go of old resentments, deliver them
up to the sky and wait—however long
it might take—for replication.

So I knelt down and thought about
my feelings toward you all those
years, sometimes hatred for what
you'd done. The guilt and control
pushing me away, pushing me forward
to the bottle where I found brief
comfort. An illusion, the excuses
I hid behind, buttons I thought you
pushed only to realize my skewed
perception screwed me up, not you.

When I finally opened my eyes—
how much time had passed, a poem—
the messenger bird flew away.
I watched as he ascended to heaven
and knew you did the best you could.

# To Mother

Waking still, I yearn
to lean on bended knee
safe within your shadow
to rest my quivering chin
in the palm of your hand
hear your comforting words—
*everything will be okay*
but flames erode your body,
immeasurable time hangs
in a white sheet, a ghost.
Will you survive
the inky slash
of one month?
Two?
The holidays a pebble
throw away, your smile
burning holes in my heart.

# Saying Goodbye

One day the top will close
   and I'll watch your coffin
      drop below Mother Earth.

I'll flood the dirt with tears
   even though I knew it was coming
      I'll know I never really did.

# About the Author

Laurie Kolp is an award-winning poet with numerous publications. Her varied style brings something for everyone, striving to touch on everyday life with compassion and thought-provoking prowess. She is part of the online communities dVerse Poets and Poetry Jam, and the vice-president of Texas Gulf Coast Writers. Laurie lives in Southeast Texas with her husband, three kids, and two dogs.

www.ingramcontent.com/pod-product-compliance
Lightning Source LLC
Chambersburg PA
CBHW021930040426
42448CB00008B/994